Flipguide

D1364297

Design

From the Industrial Revolution to the 21st Century

Designers and Companies

AEG

The "Allgemeine Deutsche Elektrizi-täts-Gesellschaft" (founded in 1883 as the German Edison Company, re-named 1887) had its origins with the farsighted engineer Emil Rathenau who in 1881 had already acquired the German patent right for the Edison bulb. For the first project undertaken by this big industry, AEG appointed an "artistic advisor", the German architect Peter Behrens, who until 1914 was con-cerned with the appearance of the products, or what is today known as "Corporate Identity". In the beginning, a combination of Jugendstil elements were combined with geometric forms, resulting in the AEG designs of the 20s being known for their cool efficiency (for instance, the "Vampyrette" vacuum cleaner with chromed steel tube). This austere style was maintained, except for an interlude of streamlined forms in the fifties, up to the Ulmer inspired school of the sixties. Today, AEG's trademark is its high quality; the chief designer is Hans Strohmeier.

Apple Macintosh

This Computer firm was founded in 1976 by Steven Paul Jobs and Stephen G. Wozniak and is as well known for its innovation regarding user-logistics as for its appearance. In 1984 the German designer Hartmut Esslinger (his firm was named Frogdesign) designed a pure white Apple computer and thereby cre-ated an optical appearance which clear-ly distinguishes the "Mac" from the uninspired beige-brown products of other companies. The user-surfaces re-flected the surroundings of the office. The latest Apple creations "iMac" and "eMate" once again set new standards for form.

Arad, Ron (born 1951, Tel Aviv)

English designer and architect of Israeli origin. Arad has lived in London since 1973; he was co-founder of the design studio Off Off (1981) and of Ron Arad Associates Ltd. (1989) for architecture and applied design as well as the Ron Arad Studios in Como, Italy (1994). He designed objects for, among others, the firms Kartell, Alessi and Artemide. His architectural works are inter alia the Opera House in Tel Aviv and the Belgo restaurant chain in London. Arad is regarded as the most important repre-sentative of "New Design" in England. He is presently professor in furniture design at the Royal College of Arts (RCA) in London.

Art Nouveau

The French term for Jugendstil, named after the gallery of art dealer Salomon Bing in Paris. Especially well-known and precious Art Nouveau objects are the jewellery pieces by the Parisian jew-eller René Lalique, like a brooch for the actress Sarah Bernhardt in the form of a dragonfly, or glass art works from the manufacturers Emile Galles and the brothers Auguste and Antoine Daum in Nancy. The magazine "Revue Blanche" was responsible for distribution of the new ideas.

Behrens, Peter (14.4.1869, Hamburg – 27.2.1940, Berlin)

Behrens was a genuine universal talent; architect, painter, graphic designer, industrial designer, book artist, callig-rapher, landscaper, draftsman. His artis-tic output includes many carpets, wall-hangings, jewellery, mounts and numerous pieces of furniture. As a founder member of the Munich Seces-sion, he first adhered to Jugendstil, but his form of expression changed after World War I towards functionalism. As architect he designed, among others, the turbine hall of the AEG firm in Berlin, where he reduced the multitude of forms to a few building elements which are technically easy to produce and can be replicated endlessly. Behrens be-longed to the German work union (Werkbund) which strove to create a general "culture of good taste".

Bialetti, Alfonso (1888–1970)

The Italian Bialetti, originally a metal worker, founded a metal workshop in

1918 in Crusinallo (Province of Novara) where he manufactured small metal domestic appliances. Due to his experience here and his knowledge of the aluminium spray technique which he acquired during his six years stay in Paris, Bialetti invented the three-part espresso jug "Moka Express". Its unique and, up till the present, unchanged design as well as its excellent quality made it a winner all over the world. After World War II Bialetti's son Renato continued with his factory and sold it in 1993 to the Rondini group, who have kept the original name.

Bill, Max (22.12 1908, Winterthur – 12.9.1994, Berlin)

Swiss painter, sculptor, architect, graphic artist, designer and art theoretician. He is considered one of the most prolific initiators of modern concrete art in post-war Europe. Bill studied at the Bauhaus in Dessau and took over the idea of joining the arts under the primacy of architecture. As exponent of Concrete art, of which Theo van Doesberg first formulated the principles in 1924, Bill based his artful creations on aesthetic norms and scientific laws which had their origin in mathematically logical constructions. Geometric elements were combined with the scientific elements of colour and thus excluded anything involuntary and accidental. In Bill's versatile creations, painting is dominant; his main architectural work is the entire complex of the High School of Design in Ulm (1950–54) which he led from 1951 to 1956. Bill has worked since 1944 as industrial and furniture designer, his first object was the typewriter Patria, which is an excellent example of Bill's "good form in products".

Brandt, Edgar (24.12.1880, Paris – 8.5.1960, Genf)

French art smith and designer. Brandt was one of the main exponents of Art Deco in France. His pieces are characterised by their clear, powerful lines, individual diversity and ornamental richness, the form is well designed without exaggeration. In 1926 Brandt founded the Société des Etablissements; to fulfill the numerous commissions he soon employed modern apparatus (e.g. welding tools for complicated ornaments) and machines. Following the designs of architects, Brandt made gates, fences, balustrades and casings for lifts: his works (e.g. the main gate on the Champs-Elysées) were the visual highlight of the Paris Expo in 1926. Brandt also worked together with glass artists such as Auguste Daum in Nancy and René Lalique. At the beginning of the 1930's Brandt created luxury wooden furniture and designed the décor for passenger liners, offices and private homes.

Brandt, Marianne (1.10.1893, Chemnitz – 18.6.1983, Kirchberg)

German designer, painter and photographer. Brandt studied from 1923 until 1925 at the state Bauhaus in Weimar, from 1927 she was an employee in the metal workshop of the Bauhaus in Dessau, from April 1928 also the deputy leader. In 1929 she received the Bauhaus diploma for the metal workshop. In 1930–1933 she was working at the metal ware factory Ruppelwerk in Gotha as designer. Brandt is renowned as one of the most important artists of the Bauhaus metal workshop: she became known mainly through her designs for industrial products of metal and glass (e.g. lamps), yet is also famous for her individual pieces (tea pots, ash trays, tea sets).

Braun AG

Founded in 1921 in Frankfurt am Main by engineer Max Braun as a workplace for the manufacture of apparatus. Today Braun AG are regarded as the leading manufacturers of small electrical appliances. Their products are known for their functional and aesthetically appealing design: The radio-gramophone combination "Sk 4" (1956) became famous and was lovingly known by the public as "Snow White's coffin". The electric razor "Braun Sixtant" which set the leading standard came on the market in 1962. Their winning colour combination of black and silver set a trend which was followed for decades by other firms – and not only for household appliances.

Breuer, Marcel (22.5.1902, Pécs– 1.7.1981, New York)

Hungarian-American architect and designer. Breuer's best known objects are the free-swinger without hind legs "B 32" and "B 64" (steel pipe, wood and cane) of 1928. Breuer studied and taught from 1920–1928 at the State Bauhaus in Weimar and Dessau, and was one of its most important and unique representatives. The aesthetics of his furniture, often with strict geometric forms and modern materials, were a direct result of their function. After completion of his studies in 1928 Breuer worked in Berlin as an independent architect; in 1933 he emigrated first to Budapest (till 1935), then to London and, lastly, the USA (1937, initiated by Walter Gropius) where he opened the architects' office M.B. and Associated Architects in New York in 1956.

Chareau, Pierre (4.8.1883, Le Havre–1950, East Hampton/USA)

French architect, interior and furniture designer. Very early Chareau distanced his furniture designs from Art Deco and developed his own unique power of expression outside of the current fashion, combining wrought iron and wood in his furniture. Together with Bernard Bijvoet he built the "Maison de verre" (1928–32), a building that, with its huge glass panels and the variability of interior spaces (turn and push doors, moveable walls, a staircase that can be drawn in), is recognised as the principal architectural work of the twenties. In the USA Chareau completed only a few projects.

Colombo, Joe (30.7.1930, Milan– 30.7.1971, Milan)

Italian painter, sculptor, designer and architect; dedicated himself from 1963 mainly to design. His first object was the lamp "Acrilia", then followed, inter alia, a small, moveable kitchen in a block ("Carrellone Mini-Kitchen"), originally conceived in cast aluminium, 1967 resulted in plastic seat furniture "Universale" as well as prototypes of rapidly mobile house structures (e.g. "Cabriolet-Bed"). Beyond that, Colombo also designed the interiors for several shops and exhibition stalls in Milan (1965–1970), at the same time he developed a lighting system with reflectors that would be affordable to the industry, namely the "Lampada Castoro". With his use of unconventional colours and the regular use of plastic material for comfortable, mass produced furniture, Colombo exerted a crucial influence on Italian furniture design of the 60s and 70s.

Conran, Sir Terence (born 4.10.1931 in Esher/Surrey)

English interior decorator, ceramist, furniture and textile designer. In 1964 Conran opened the first Habitat furniture shop and in the 70s he founded, together with Sean Sutcliffe, the furniture workshop Benchmark. His textile designs show elegant patterns from organic elements, often plants or flowers in rhythmic arrangements or abstract, colourful designs. His furniture designs are determined by a love of detail and the use of natural materials and colours (metal, cane, mainly lighter wood). Conran's second passion is gastronomy, from 1952 he opened several restaurants, hotels or cafés of a superior class and published cook books. His contribution in the 60s was to give the English middle-class a renewed sense of form and function, in the tradition of the Arts-and-Crafts movement

D'Ascanio, Corradino 1.2.1897, Popoli–1981, Pisa)

Italian engineer and aeroplane engineer. D'Ascanio, from 1915–1918 was a pilot in the Italian airforce, constructed not only the first helicopter of the world

(1930), but also designed the legendary "Vespa" scooter for the Piaggio company. The one-piece body reminded one with its flowing form of a helicopter, its streamlined form of car design in the USA, where D'Ascario worked in the Pomilio aeroplane factory in Indianapolis. Besides a number of "Vespa" models, D'Ascario developed the helicopters "P. D. 3" and "P. D. 4".

De Pas – D'Urbino – Lomazzi
The offices founded in 1966 by the architects and designers Jonathan De Pas, Donato D'Urbino and Paolo Lomazzi, attracted attention at the end of the sixties with inflatable objects such as the easy chair "Blow" (1967) which was designed for the Zanotta company, or inflatable houses for the Italian pavilion at the exposition in Osaka. In 1972 the group took part in the exhibition "Italy: The New Domestic Landscape" at the Museum of Modern Art in New York. Their contribution to the exhibition "Italienische Möbel Design 1950/80" in the city museum in Cologne consisted of objects that lingered on the border between architecture and design. In 1979 the Compasso d'Oro prize was awarded to them. As directors of the Industrial Design Association, De Pas, D'Urbino and Lomazzi also made a name for themselves by their theoretical contributions. Since the death of Jonathan De Pas in 1991, the company is led by D'Urbino and Lomazzi and widely recognized under the name DDL Studio.

Dresdner Werkstätten für Handwerkskunst
In 1900 under the influence of the English Arts-and-Crafts movement, a real upsurge of ambitious craft traders, including the Dresdner workshops in Germany, took place. Under the leadership of Karl Schmidt craftsmen, artists and architects made furniture and household equipment of unusually simple aesthetics. Well known draftsmen were Richard Riemerschmid and Bruno Paul. In 1907 the Dresdner workshops joined forces with the Vereinigten Werkstätten and the Werkstätten für Wohnungseinrichtung – both in Munich – to form a big company which had an own factory and managed retailing points across the whole of Germany under the name of Deutsche Werkstätte. The most famous project is the Garden city Hellerau with work places, living quarters, gym school and festive hall (started in 1909), designed by Heinrich Tessenow and Richard Riemerschmid, a social reform collective work of art of which the restoration was undertaken during the past few years.

Drocco, Guido (born 1942)
Italian architect and designer. Drocco is first and foremost an architect who participated in projects like the rebuilding of the Lingotto Fiat Works in Turin (1983), as well as the building of the office block Uffici Giudiziari in Alba (1982–1987). As designer he was known especially for the inflatable hallstand "Cactus", designed in 1971 in conjunction with Franco Mello for the Italian firm Gufram. Drocco is currently a lecturer at the faculty of architecture at the Technical High School in Turin.

D'Urbino, Donato (born 1935)
See De Pas – D'Urbino – Lomazzi

Eames, Charles Ormand (17.6. 1907, St. Louis–21.8.1978, St. Louis)
American architect and designer. Eames was one of the leading exponents of American design in the forties and fifties. He became internationally known in 1940, when, together with Eero Saarinen, he won the "Organic Design in Home Furnishing" competition of the Museum of Modern Art in New York. In conjunction with his second wife Ray, he made other furniture ("Lounge Chair" 1956), developed toys (building block systems), designed exhibitions, and showed films (e.g. "Black Top", 1950). To Eames, a precise analysis of the design problem of the moment

was important, and he thus constantly sought new technologies and materials (e.g. fibre glass) with which to solve these problems. Eames' most significant architectural work, his home in Santa Monica, California, portrayed his style through its optical lightness.

Ford Motor Company

Engineer Henry Ford (1863–1947) founded the Ford Motor Company in Detroit, Michigan in 1903 and in 1909 he introduced the legendary "Model T". The affordable, light, but also robust car became an enormous public success. Ford's next revolutionary development was the assembly line in 1913, that allowed for the exact completion of more cars. Yet the production of the stylistically almost unchanged "Tin Lizzie", which was only available in black, had to be ceased in 1927 when the "Ford A" hit the market. The General Motors company became a powerful opponent to Mr. Ford by annually introducing aesthetically pleasing models in a variety of forms and colours.

Frankfurter Küche

The first built-in kitchen for cluster housing was developed by the Austrian architect Grete Schütte-Lihotzky in Frankfurt am Main in 1926. Extreme economy in the division of the room, short paths and the streamlining of house tasks were the main considerations for the concept of the modern small kitchen.

Functionalism

Functionalism is the reduction of form to the most essential elements by omitting decorative frills; the use of modern materials, longevity and high quality products, as well as the installation of industrial processes for production. This idea points in some way to the red thread that runs through the history of German design: Starting with the establishment of the Deutschen Werkbund in 1907, continued and strengthened by the social reform goals of Bauhaus, and re-introduced after World War I by the

Ulmer School, it has continued to this day, except for a short interlude in the eighties, in the work of younger designers such as Konstantin Grcic or Axel Kufus

Gallé, Emile (4.5.1846, Nancy– 23.9.1904, Nancy)

French glass and ceramic artist. Gallé is one of the most renowned exponents of the French Jugendstil (Art Nouveau) in the area of manual arts. Especially well known are his cameo glasses, vases of different colored layers, in which ornamental reliefs are cut by means of various grinding processes. During 1987 Gallé changed to the new, very complicated technique of "Marqueterie verre" a type of inlay work in glass. For the ornamental décor of his artistic glass, influenced by Japan, he undertook extensive studies of nature. The wide treasure of forms in nature had a definite influence on his designs for furniture. Original and extremely precious are his "Meubles parlants" with inlaid lines from poems or proverbs. For many decades after his death the workshop Gallé produced work, yet never equaling the quality of the master.

Gatti, Piero (born 1940, Turin)

Italian architect and designer. In 1965 Piero Gatti, together with Cesare Paolini and Franco Teodoro established an office in Turin. Besides being architects and industrial designers they ventured into the fields of city planning, decoration, product development, graphic design and photography. Their armchair "Sacco" (1968/69 for the firm Zanotta), a leather bag filled with polystyrene balls, won the designer prize Compasso d'Oro and can be seen in many museums in Europe and America. Cezare Paolini died in 1983.

Gaultier, Jean Paul (born 1952, Arcueil)

French fashion designer. Gaultier began his career in 1970 as assistant to Pierre Cardin; in 1976 he opened his own fashion house. He experimented in his collection with the widest range of materials and daring colour combinations, which always caused sensation. During the mid-eighties he introduced fashion for men which included skirts, net stockings and high heels. His 1990 corset-costume for Madonna's show is a legend. Since the beginning of the nineties Gaultier also designs articles for everyday use as well as furniture.

Graves, Michael
(born 1934, Indianapolis)

American architect and designer. Graves studied architecture at the universities of Cincinnati and Harvard and was professor in architecture at Princeton University. He designed furniture and articles for daily use. Famous is his series of water kettle (1985), cream jug (1988) and sugar bowl (1988), which he made for the firm of Alessi. "In the personal language of the forms of Michael Graves, the stimulation from European tradition, Art Deco, American Pop and elements from pre-Columbian cultures are combined." (Alberto Alessi, 1999).

Gray, Eileen (9.8.1878, Enniscorthy–28.11.1976, Paris)

Irish designer. Until 1930 Gray, who originally studied painting, made mainly laquered works and furniture, which she sold from her own small Parisian shop to wealthy private clients. In the years 1927–1929 she built her own house in Rocquebrune (with the support of her friend and mentor, the Romanian architect Jean Badovici) for which she also designed the furniture, including her most famous piece, the "E 1027" – a table with adjustable height. Grays creations, although inclined to be functional, are charming because of their variability and elegance and are less formal than the steel pipe furniture of many of her colleagues.

Gropius, Walter (18.5.1883, Berlin–5.7.1969, Boston)

German architect and industrial designer, founder and leader of the state Bauhaus in Weimar and Dresden (until 1928). Gropius' aim was a synthesis of all art forms under the umbrella of architecture, the "Einheitskunstwerk" – a macro construction – in which no boundaries exist between monumental and decorative art. The idea of integration was contained in the curriculum of the Bauhaus: famous is the "Vorkurs" the basic education of students in various disciplines concerned with research in materials and formal laws, and was conditional for specialisation in the different work places. For Gropius design meant the "symbiosis of art and technology"; through industrial manufacturing and new materials a wide mass of affordable, aesthetically pleasing domestic items should be made available to the masses. In 1933 Gropius went first to England where he actualised various architectural projects and thereafter in 1936 he became a professor at Harvard and shortly before opening his own office with his friend Marcel Breuer. In 1955 he again executed commissions in Germany (e.g. plans for a settlement in Britz-Buckow, Berlin, later called Gropius city). Gropius' influence on architecture and design in the 20th century can scarcely be overrated.

Gugelot, Hans (1.4.1920, Kamassar/Indonesia–9.10.1965, Ulm)

Dutch architect and product designer. After his engineering and architectural studies in Switzerland Gugelot worked together with Max Bills from 1948–1950; in 1950 he opened his own office and developed the furniture-element system "M125". In 1954 Bill called him to the "Hochschule für Gestaltung" (HfG) in Ulm, where Gugelot taught design from 1955 and led the "Development Group II". In the same year Braun, the electric appliance company, commissioned him for the development of designs for new products, for which he received the Grand Prix at the XI Triennale in Milan. In 1955/56 he developed, together with Dieter Rams, the legendary radio-gramophone combination "SK4" (known as "Snow

White's Coffin), and in 1961 with Gerd Alfred Müller the famous electric razor "Braun Sixtant". These appliances made Gugelot one of the best known protagonists of the "less is more" philosophy. From 1960 Gugelot had his own production firm.

Guimard, Hector (10.3.1867, Paris–20.5.1942, New York)

French architect, interior architect and designer. One of the most important exponents of Art Nouveau. He became famous as a result of the construction of the entrances to the Paris Métro Stations (from 1899) with their curved abstract-organic lines, which introduced the name "Style Métro" or "Style Guimard" into the French Jugendstil. Besides his work as architect Guimard designed a variety of furniture, wall paper and ceramics (for the porcelain factory Sèvres). After 1910 he changed to a simpler, more functional style. In 1938 he moved to the USA.

Good Form

This concept goes back to an exhibition of Max Bill (1949; 1957 published in book form) and is the same as the American "Good Design", the English "Contemporary Style" and the Swedish "Nyttokonst". Good Form was measured by the following criteria: high consumer value and durability, timelessness and simplicity, safety and good manufacturing. The innovative demands in the fifties (especially in Scandinavia) that rationality should determine the appearance of products, became rigid dogma in the sixties. The present day "federal price product design" in Germany can be traced back to the "federal price Good Form" which was created in 1969.

Haslocher Tischfabrik

The extendable table and furniture factory (today GmbH) which Richard August Hainke started after World War I is still regarded as one of the most important table and chair manufacturers in Germany. For many internationally re-nowned hotels such as the Interconti-nental in Paris, the Four Seasons in Munich or Kempinski in Berlin, this company has designed and fitted out their interiors. Numerous pieces from the Hainke-collection have been patented since the fifties. In 1954 the Haslocher factory produced the kidney-shaped table which became a status symbol in German lounges.

Henningsen, Poul (1894, Kopenhagen–1967, Kopenhagen)

Danish architect, light designer, writer, composer of songs and producer. Henningsen, "PH" for short, was an institution in Denmark – his ideas for design and objects, but also because of his social engagement which had an important influence. His main interest was the electric light: in 1924 he developed his first lamp which evolved over the following years into the "PH" lamp which doesn't blind you. To obtain focused distribution of light, he used scientific analysis, yet at the same time his lamps were aimed at mass production and were thus readily available. They consisted of cleverly intertwined shades and caused striking aesthetic patterns in the room. His "snake chair" of the early thirties consisted of one twisted piece of pipe.

Hitchcock, Henry-Russell (born 1903)

In 1932, together with Philip C. Johnson, Hitchcock published the document "The International Style: Architecture since 1922" for the exhibition by the same name at the Museum of Modern Art in New York, from which the International Style in the thirties and fifties derived its name.

Hochschule für Gestaltung (HfG) Ulm

Although the HfG only lasted a few years, it exercised a considerable influence on design in the second half of the twentieth century. The American army of occupation started it in 1947 as a "re-education" institution and it was established by Inge Scholl (the sister of Hans and Sophie Scholl), Otl Aicher (the creator of the stick figure comic strips for the Munich Olympics in 1972) and Max Bill. The college was opened in 1955. With functionalism, a belief in progress, the consideration of social factors, and the interdisciplinary perspectives (compulsory for all students), the traditions of the Bauhaus were continued. In 1956 the Argentine Tomas Maldonado succeeded Max Bill as director and developed the empirical-positive concept of the "Ulmer model", which not only advocated the ideas for design theory and solid methods, but also close cooperation with industry through the development of "product systems": the "Development department 11" became famous under Hans Gugelot. In 1968 the HfG was closed because of political pressure and cuts in funding.

Jacobsen, Arne (11.2.1902, Kopenhagen–24.3.1971, Kopenhagen)

Danish architect, furniture and product designer. Jacobsen's three-legged chair "Myren" (ants) of 1952 became well-known, not only for its timelessness and high quality, but also for its unusual versatility. To date, more than five million units have been sold. Jacobsen's designs originated mostly in conjunction with concrete building projects, like the frequently copied easy chair, "Svanen" (swan) and "ægett" (egg) with their twisted forms which Jacobsen designed for the SAS Royal Hotel in Copenhagen. He was also commissioned to design the interior of this hotel.

Jeanneret, Pierre 22.3.1896, Geneva–4.12.1967, Geneva)

Swiss architect and designer. Jeanneret is primarily known as partner to his cousin Le Corbusier, together with whom he designed a series of buildings in the 20s such as the houses created by them in a rural settlement in Stuttgart, the cluster houses La Roche and Jeanneret-Raaf in Auteuil or the Pavillon des Esprit Nouveau in Paris. In 1928 he, Le Corbusier and Charlotte Perriand designed a collection of steel pipe furniture that was displayed at the Salon d'automne the following year. In 1946 an end to the collaboration with Le Corbusier came about. In the meantime Jeanneret worked as architect, city planner and designer mainly in Switzerland and France.

Johnson, Philip Cortelyou (born 8.7.1906, Cleveland)

American architect. As leader of the architectural department at the Museum of Modern Art, he and Henry-Russell Hitchcock compiled the exhibition catalogue "The International Style" which lent international style its name in 1932. From 1940 until 1943 he studied architecture with Walter Gropius and Marcel Breuer in Harvard and worked there as an independent architect from 1942. Until 1956 his style was visibly influenced by Mies van der Rohe with whom he also collaborated in the construction of the Seagram building in New York (1954–1958). Then Johnson gave up on functional seriousness and entered a playful mannerist phase in the sixties before going over to monumental forms (e.g. Art Hall Bielefeld 1968). Today he is considered one of the main exponents of post-modernism.

"Die Jugend" (1896–1940)

Illustrated German cultural publication and the channel which gave Jugendstil its name, founded by Munich publishers and writer Georg Hirth. In other countries magazines were also responsible for the spreading of the ideas of the New Style; in Austria "Ver Sacrum", in France the "Revue Blanche", in England the "Yellow Books", published by Aubrey Beardsley. Other important German publications were the "Simplicissimus" (München), "Pan" (Berlin) as well as "Kunst und Dekoration" (Darmstadt.)

Kartell

This enterprise was founded by the Italian chemist and engineer Giulio Castelli in 1949, and was intended to make small, affordable kitchen appliances from plastic. Lemon presses, a pasta sieve, waste bins, boxes and other kitchen utensils all suddenly appeared in special forms and colours which could mainly be attributed to the designer Gino Colombini. The pioneering work in the laboratories of Kartell introduced the decade of synthetic material for furniture at the beginning of the sixties. The high chair "K 4999" as designed by Marco Zanuso and Richard Sapper in 1961 and manufactured in 1964, showed that it was now a technical possibility to make plastic furniture with enough rigidity and synthetic material thus became acceptable for interior design. At the same time, people who advocated its use like Anna Castelli Ferrieri, Joe Colombo, Vico Magistretti or Giotto Stoppino, and later young designers like Phillipe Starck or Ron Arad, created with this material for experimental pleasure and its unusual combinations and thus set the trend for furniture production.

King, Perry A. (born 1938)

British designer. In the sixties King went to Italy as product designer where he worked with Ettore Sottsass. Their portable typewriter "Valentine", which was designed for Olivetti in 1969 became famous. Together with Santiago, Miranda King runs the studio, King-Miranda, which designs furniture and office interiors.

Constructivism

A non-objective trend in fine and applied arts of the 20th century which originated in Russia and was influenced by the ideas of socialist transformation in society. Constructivism, according to El Lissitzky, did not create any abstraction (of impressions of nature), but should, on the basis of geometric elements objectively, and without any personal feelings, construct objects which display scientific observations and technical achievements.

Lalique, René (6.4.1860, L'Hayles-Roses—1.5.1945, Paris)

French glass and jewellery artist. As goldsmith, Lalique set new standards for jewellery design in that his pieces copied elements of nature (peacocks, dragon flies, vegetables) and new materials for that time such as semi-precious stones, mother-of-pearl and enamel were used. Also in glass art (perfume bottles, vases, lights) he ventured into new realms: his objects are often "iced" or in relief on the surface.

Lomazzi, Paolo (born 1936)

See De Pas – D'Urbino – Lomazzi

Le Corbusier (6.10.1887, La-Chaux-de Fonds—27.8.1965, Roquebrune-Cap-Martin)

French-Swiss architect, city planner, designer, painter and sculptor, actually Charles-Edouard Jeanneret-Gris. Le Corbusier's concepts and his simple and functional buildings with flat roofs and large windows had a marked influence on architecture in the 20th century. He developed a new building style in reinforced concrete constructions, by replacing support walls with a system of stanchions, which allowed more freedom in the ground-plan. Houses, shops and other buildings essential to life should be reduced to "living machines" (Unité d'Habitation in Marseille, 1945–1949). Le Corbusier's late work, the pilgrim's church of Ronchamp (1950–1955), did not interest itself with geometric forms, but rather showed preference for graphic portrayals. His furniture, all of which became classic pieces, combines functionality and simple form with elegance and refinement, e.g. the hide-covered Chaise-longue "LC4" (1928) which he developed together with Pierre Jeanneret and Charlotte Perriand.

Lissitzky, El (23.11.1880, Potschinok–30.12.1941, Moscow)

Russian-Soviet painter, graphic designer, photographer, architect and art theorist, actually Eliezer Markovich Lissizky. As one of the most important exponents of Constructivism, Lissitzky contributed much to the distribution of this idea to central Europe and especially Germany:1922–1923 he worked in Amsterdam, Berlin and Hannover, made and extended his contacts with the De-Stijl group and Bauhaus. The task of constructional art is, according to him, not to adorn life but to organise it. Lissitzky's ideas had a definite influence on the art of printing; he designed posters, advertisements (e.g. for the Pelican company) and typographical concepts. In 1925–1928 he made a name for himself as designer for exhibitions; he designed the abstract spaces for the modern cabinet in the Landesmuseum in Hannover. In 1928 he returned to the Soviet Union where he was commissioned by the government to be responsible for Russian art exhibitions abroad. Later, he was the architect in charge of Gorki Park. With his photographic work and experiments he had an influence on Russian avantgarde photography.

Loewy, Raymond (5.11.1893, Paris–14.7.1986, Monte Carlo)

American industrial designer of French origin. No single person had such an influence on the American image as Loewy. In 1919 he immigrated to the USA and worked in New York as window dresser and illustrator for fashion magazines such as "Vogue". From the thirties he designed diverse models of Studebakers (1938–1962), Greyhound busses (1940), the packaging for "Lucky Strike" cigarettes (1941) which is still in use today, and the Shell Corporate Identity (1968–1972). NASA (since 1967) commissioned him to design the inner space of the Apollo space capsule as well as the Skylab space station.

Lomonossow-Porcelain-Manufactory

This St Petersburg based firm has existed since 1744. In the time after the October revolution this company endeavoured to find technical solutions to mass production. The décor of the time was geared to the avant garde "Agitpropkunst", and the designs followed the ideas of Constructivism and Suprematism. Examples from the Lomonossow-Porcelain-Manufactory won many prizes at international expo especially in the twenties, such as a gold medal at the World Expo in Paris 1925. Today the collection has a wide spectrum of different porcelain objects.

Loos, Adolf (10.12.1870, Brünn–23.8.1933, Kalksberg)

Austrian architect, publisher and designer. In his paper of 1908 entitled "Ornament und Verbrechen" he set out the reasons for this preference for a factual style and an absence of any décor. Loos was supporter of the motto construed by his American colleague Louis Sullivan, "form follows function". With his buildings such as the Café Museum in Vienna (1899), Loos was a forerunner of the stern formality of functionalism. He also designed numerous pieces of furniture and lights, such as the table lamp "Villa Steiner"(1910)

Mackintosh, Charles Rennie (6.7.1868, Glasgow–10.12.1928, London)

Scottish architect and furniture designer. Mackintosh made a big contribution to British and European design of the 20th century. At first mainly working as an architect, he created a modern style in conjunction with his wife Margaret McDonald, Herbert McNair and Frances McDonald ("The Glasgow Four"). This style combined straight forms and elements of nature (abstracted plant and animal motifs) with Celtic motifs. His buildings with their interiors, such as the Hill House in Helensburgh (1903) are consummate works of art in themselves where every detail counts.

Mackmurdo, Arthur Heygate (1851–1942)

British architect, decorator and furniture designer. Mackmurdo studied architecture with James Brooks and attended drawing classes with John Ruskin who greatly influenced him. Like the Arts-and-Crafts movement of William Morris, he established the Century Guild in 1882, a coming together of artists and craftsmen with the same objectives. The group designed furniture, metal objects, wallpaper, enamel work and textiles. Mackmurdo is seen as the forerunner of art nouveau in England. From 1900 his work as designer took up most of his time, yet few of these works have survived.

Mello, Franco

Italian designer. Created in 1971 together with Guido Drocco the inflatable hall stand "Cactus" for the Italian firm Gufram.

Memphis

The association which was founded by Jochen Gros, Ettore Sottsass and other designers in 1980 opposed the formula "form follows function" which dominated European design from the twenties. Sottsass stated the following concerning the significance of this group and their goals: "Memphis' function is to exist". The Memphis designer approached the planning of objects with a playful, intuitive and emotional attitude, making them appear "crazy" to many: expression in the form of individual, unfolding personalities.

Mendini, Alessandro (born 1931, Milan)

Italian architect, designer, publisher and theorist. Mendini, an architect from home, is seen as one of the most creative and unconventional heads of modern Italian design. As implacable opponent of functionalism and rules of industrial productivity, ornamentation and décor play a distinctive role in Mendini's designs. "To design is to decorate", said the philosopher of the group, Studio Alchimia, which was founded in 1976. His curved kitchen appliances in pastel colours (1996) which he designed for Phillips/Alessi demonstrate clearly that the old principle "form follows function" has been replaced with the motto "form follows fiction" in the later Italian design.

Mies van der Rohe, Ludwig (27.3.1886, Aachen–17.8.1969, Chicago)

German-American architect and furniture designer, actually Ludwig Mies (Rohe was the name of his mother). The son of a bricklayer, he worked from 1905 as a furniture draftsmen in the studio of Bruno Paul and from 1908 in Peter Behrens' architects office. In 1912 he opened his own architectural office in Berlin (until 1937). He soon designed reinforced concrete structures; the New York Seagram building (1954–1958) and the Berlin National Gallery (1962–1965) became particularly famous. His fame as a designer started with the steel pipe-freeswinger ("MR-Chair"– 1927) without back legs whose basic construction principle he usurped from the Dutch architect Mart Stam (which led to a court battle lasting many years); the use of steel pipe instead of wood was an idea of Marcel Breuer. Many pieces of furniture by Mies van der Rohe originated as mere by-products of his building commissions, thus he designed the "MR-Chair" at a time when he led the project of the Stuttgart "Weißenhof" settlement (1972) and the "Barcelona-chair" for the German pavilion at the International exhibition in Barcelona (1929). From 1930 Mies was the leader of the Bauhaus, the closing down of which (1932) he could, however, not prevent. In 1938 he immigrated to the USA and realised many building projects all over the World. Walter Gropius, Marcel Breuer and Mies are regarded as important masters of the "International Style".

Moggridge, Bill (born 1943)

English product designer. Born as an

Englishman, he moved to Palo Alto, California in 1977 where he worked for the electronics industry. A milestone was the design of the world's first laptop ("Compass", 1982, for the Grid Company), however, his biggest breakthrough came in 1988 with the creation of the Microsoft Mouse. In 1991 Moggridge founded the firm IDEO Product Development in San Francisco (with David Kelley and Mike Nutall), who were selected in 1996 by the design centre in Nordrhein-Westfalen as "Design Group of the Year". In 1988 he designed the electronic "Soft-book".

Moholy-Nagy, Lászlo (20.7.1895, Bácsborsod–24.11.1946, Chicago)

Hungarian painter, sculptor, commercial artist, typographer, stage designer, writer and art teacher. The multi-talented Moholy is one of the key figures of Bauhaus. He spent 1923–1928 developing the discourse for his own pedagogical concept of education; as leader of the metal workshop he encouraged students like Marianne Brandt and Marcel Breuer to produce their, now famous, designs. He himself was interested in photo graphical experiments and development of mobile light sculptures. Maholy felt himself bound by the principles of constructivism and developed a modern terminology, especially in his Bauhaus books, which were published again through his efforts. In 1929 he left the Bauhaus, created a number of stage designs in Berlin which attracted much attention and immigrated in 1937 to Chicago where he founded the "New Bauhaus".

Mollino, Carlo (6.5.1905, Turin–27.8.1973, Turin)

Italian architect, engineer, photographer and designer. The eccentric Mollino was a true multi-talent. His work encompasses nearly all the disciplines of fine and applied arts. As researcher he held twelve patent rights, but was also internationally renowned as a skier and racing driver. His furniture boasts swelling organic forms, quite often imitating the anatomy of women, which bear no relation to cold rationalism, yet at the same time are extremely precise in their construction. One of his best known objects is the sofa table "Arabesque" which he designed in the early fifties.

Morris, William (24.3.1834, Walthamstow–3.10.1896, Hammersmith)

British furniture and textile designer, social reformer, painter and writer. Morris demanded the revival of arts and crafts, the self determined authentic work in place of machine made objects. Morris' designs for furniture, material and wallpaper were extremely radical for his time, because they set the "truth to materials" in place of the illusionary effects of historicism. Thus Morris accentuated the flatness of material in his floral and mainly symmetrical designs on wallpaper. The Arts-and-Crafts movement which Morris initiated and led, had a considerable influence on the architecture and design of the 19th century and well into the 20th century.

Paolini, Cesare (1937, Genua–1983, Turin)

See Gatti, Piero

Perriand, Charlotte (1903, Paris–27.10.1999, Paris)

French architect and designer. After completion of her studies of interior design at the Ecole l'Unison Centrale des Arts Décoratifs in Paris she worked for ten years in the studio of Le Corbusier and Pierre Jeanneret (1927–1937). She was part of the famous set of steel pipe furniture, to which the recliner "LC 4" belongs. In 1940–1946 she stayed in Japan. On her return to France she became a successful interior designer. She was responsible for projects such as the presentation of conference halls for the UNO in Gent (1959–1970) or the furnishing of the of the Japanese Consulate residence in Paris (1965). At the end of the seventies she oversaw the manufacture of the Le Corbusier furniture at Cassina.

Piretti, Giancarlo
(born 8.6.1940, Bologna)

Italian furniture designer. Since 1960 Piretti has worked for the Bolognese furniture restorer Castelli, whose research and development department he heads. From 1963–1970 he taught interior design at the Instituto Statale d'Arte in Bologne. In 1969 he successfully managed the design of the folding chair. The "Plia" (for Castelli) was an absolute combination of aesthetics and functionality and as a result has become a much copied classical piece.

Rams, Dieter
(born 20.5.1932, Wiesbaden)

German architect and designer. After his architectural and interior decoration studies in Wiesbaden, Rams worked in the architectural offices of Otto Appel in Frankfurt am Main between 1953–1955. In 1955 he changed to the Braun firm and became the head designer in 1961. Rams became famous for designing, together with Hans Gugelot, the Radio-Phonogram "SK4" ("Snow White's coffin"). As furniture designer, he developed the "wall unit system 606" (1960) and the "Armchair 620" (1962), both for Otto Zapf (today Wiese Vitsoe), Eschborn. From 1987–1997 Ram was president of the Council of Design, the only institution for design in Germany.

Rietveld, Gerrit Thomas (24.6.1888, Utrecht–25.6.1964, Utrecht)

Dutch architect and furniture designer. Rietveld's furniture design in wood and steel had an important influence on the Bauhaus. One of his earliest creations, the "red-blue chair" of 1917/18, became very renowned. From 1919, as a member of the De-Stijl group, Rietveld built, together with Truus Schröder-Schräder, the Rietveld-Schröder house in Utrecht in 1924; its plain construction and perfect harmony between exterior architecture and interior design made it a masterpiece of functionalism. Rietveld's last project was the Rijks Museum van Gogh in Amsterdam (1963–1973), that was completed by his colleagues.

Ritzenhoff

The glassware factory from Marsberg in Sauerland surprised the professional world at the beginning of the nineties, when it produced, together with Studio Sieger Design (a family enterprise of Dieter Sieger and his sons Christian and Michael), a series of glasses for drinking milk. On the enormous success of these glasses the firm built their strategy of pressuring top international designers to help with their collections. Since 1999 Ritzenhoff has, besides glassware, also had clocks, textiles and household objects on their programme.

Roericht, Hans (born 1930)

German product and furniture designer. Studied 1955–1959 at the College for Design in Ulm, his final work being the stackable crockery "TC 100" for the firm Rosenthal (1961). Afterwards he worked with on, among other things, on the development of the visual picture at the opening of the Olympic Games in Munich. In 1973 Roericht became professor at the College of Arts, Berlin. Roericht worked for the firms Bosch-Siemens, Loewe and Wilkhahn.

Rosenthal, AG

The porcelain firm Rosenthal in Selb was the first enterprise worldwide to maintain a designer shopchain: In the "Rosenthal Studio houses" (the first was opened in Nürnberg in 1960) the fastidious client can obtain the complete range of designs of the "Studio line"; Walter Gropius, Hans Roericht and Luigi Colani are a few of the famous names

Saarinen, Eero (20.8.1910 Kirkkonummi–1.9.1961, Ann Arbor)

Finnish-American designer and architect. Saarinen studied sculpting in Paris and architecture at Yale University; he also worked in the architect's office of his father, Eliel Saarinen (1873–1950), where he took over the leadership in 1950. At first strongly influenced by Mies van der Rohe, after 1945 Saarinen's buildings expressed creative, experimental joy (e.g. the reception hall of the Dulles International Airport in Washington D.C., 1958–1963). As furniture designer Saarinen caused excitement with the "Tulip Chair" of 1956.

Sapper, Richard
(born 30.5.1930, Munich)

German product and furniture designer. After his studies (philosophy, graphic design, engineering, economy), Sapper worked in the design department of Daimler-Benz in Stuttgart before he settled in Italy in 1958. There he worked for the department chain Rinascente and the firms Fiat, Pirelli and Alessi (e.g. Water kettle "9090" 1983). From his collaboration with Marco Zanuso (1959–1975) originated the television sets "Algol", "Doney" and "Black" (for the firm Brionvega). From 1996–1998 Sapper was professor for Industrial Design at the Art Academy of Stuttgart. At the beginning of the nineties he created the elegant notebook "Thinkpad 700 C" for IBM. Sapper's most famous creation is the adjustable table lamp "Tizio" – a masterful synthesis of aesthetics and functionality – which he designed in 1972.

Schreiner, Frank
See Stiletto

Schütte-Lihotzky (23.1.1897, Vienna–18.1.2000, Vienna)

Austrian architect. She was the first and only woman to study architecture at the K.K. College of Arts and Crafts (now the College for Applied Arts) from 1915–1919. At the beginning of the twenties she worked with Adolf Loos for the settlement cooperative in Vienna. In 1926 Ernst May invited her to Frankfurt am Main where she designed her famous "Frankfurter Küche" (kitchen). From 1933 she worked in the Soviet Union and Turkey and in 1940 decided to return to Austria to join in the active resistance against the Nazi regime. After a few weeks she was arrested and imprisoned until 1945. After the war she at first encountered many difficulties in finding employment in Vienna, being a member of the Communist Party of Austria, but in the eighties many awards came her way. In her numerous obituaries she was referred to as the "leading architect" of Austria.

Sheraton, Thomas
(1751, Stockton-on-Tees–22.10.1806, London)

English furniture draftsman. In 1791 and 1794 Sheraton published the double compilation "The Cabinet-maker and Upholsterer's Drawing Book"; in 1803 the "Cabinet Dictionary"; and in 1805 "The Cabinet-maker, Upholsterer and General Artist's Encyclopedia" (uncompleted). The detailed presentation showed Sheraton's love for decor and a well developed sense of proportion. His furniture is fine and elegant with inlays and paintings. Sheraton's designs later had an influence on furniture repair in England, northern Europe and America. Whether he ever made any pieces of furniture himself is unclear since very little is known about his life.

Sony

This Japanese firm, established in 1946 by Akio Morita, is one of the leading manufacturers of entertainment electronics. In contrast to the majority of European firms, Sony has a permanently appointed design team whose members choose to remain anonymous. In 1959 Sony developed the first portable battery driven transistor television in the world, which won a gold medal at the Milan Triennial in 1960. Further technical innovations followed like the first private video recorder (1964), the invention of the digital compact disc (together with Philips, on the market in 1980) and the legendary

"Walkman" with its steel colour and distinct angular shape.

Sottsass, Ettore (born 14.9.1917, Innsbruck)

Italien architect, furniture and industrial designer. Sottsass is one of the key figures of the later Italian design, who distanced themselves from functional principles and in its place turned to a multicoloured, cheerful style and mix of materials. "For me design is a way of discussing life, social cohesion, politics, food and even design itself", wrote Sottsass in the eighties when he suddenly became internationally renowned along with the group "Memphis" that he founded. Sottsass' best-known creations are the portable typewriter "Olivetti Valentine" in bright red (1959, together with Perry A. King) and the bookshelf "Carlton" (1981) with its colourful laminates.

Starck, Phillipe-Patrick (born 18.1.1949, Paris)

French designer, architect and interior designer. That Starck is one of the most creative French designers of today he has proved time and again: be it with the interior of the Café Costes in Paris (1984), the legendary round armchair "Costes"(1982) which has often been copied and made him famous overnight, or with the juice extractor the "Juicy Salif". While some people thought that the lack of conventional construction was a sign of a creative mind, others, for the same reason regarded the "Juicy Salif" as useless rubbish.

Stiletto (born 1959, Rüsselsheim, real name Frank Schreiner)

German sculptor and designer. Stiletto became famous through his ready-made seats "Consumer's Rest (1983) that consisted of a converted shopping trolley with only a few adjustments. The "design practitioner" who was originally inspired by the Berlin subculture proclaimed "the visibility of progress" to be his motto. In the nineties Stiletto designed mainly simple, cheap lamps such as the "Glühwürmchen" (glow worm 1990) or the "poor person's chandelier" (1999).

Straka, Sighard (born 1954)

German development engineer in the car industry. Received the iF Product Design Award in 1999 for the "Ciro" (City-Roller), the prototype of the compact scooter (of the manufacturers of sport equipment K2), known today as "Kickboard". "A product that has been known to everybody since childhood was altered here using new materials to make a fun toy for young and old alike, but can also be further developed for exhibitions or large offices", the reason given by the jury of the industrial forum in Hannover. New in comparison to the well-known children's rollerblades are the four bearings in the PU wheels which make them stable on curves and safe to ride.

Studio Alchimia

Gallery and design group in Milan. Established in 1976 by the Milanese gallery owner, architect and design theorist Alessandro Gurriero, the goal is to unite a number of known designers such as Allessandro Mendini and Ettore Sottsass. Characteristic for the group is the almost free handling of materials and forms and the playful-ironic redesigning of classic things. Studio Alchima had a big influence on Nuovo Design and was a forerunner of the commercially successful Memphis group.

Suprematism

The concept (from "Suprematie" – supremacy) was introduced round 1913 by the Russian constructivist artist Kasimir Malevich (1878–1935). For Malevich nature was free from any goalsetting and logic and this all-pervasive law he tried to carry over to art: Art can only have itself as contents and can only relate to itself, like the single elements in a structure have to relate to one another. Suprematism expelled everything expressive or narrative and only made use of plain geometrical elements such as a square, circle, ellipse, trapeze, diagonal, etc. Most radical was that Malevich illustrated his theory with the famous painting "Black square on a white surface" (1915, St Petersburg, Russian Museum).

Swatch Watches
Out of the crisis in the Swiss watch industry in the years 1970 eventually grew the Swatch Group in 1988, a renamed Swiss enterprise under the leadership of Nicolas Hayek. In the spring of 1983 the so-called unisex models were first shown which, in their further development, changed the traditional image of the wrist watch from a common product to a collector's item. Revolutionary was not only that this affordable plastic watch which was universally acceptable consisted of only 51 working parts, but that the "Swatch" served as a miracle in micro-precision and matrix technique. "The only unchanging fact about the Swatch is that it always changes" – as a result of this trend, the Swiss company artists and designers such as Franco Bosisio, Alessandro Mendini or Matteo Thun have designed about 70 different styles since 1984. Special prestige editions, e.g. by Keith Harring were also brought out.

Tatlin, Vladimir Jevgrafovich (28.12.1885, Moscow–31.5.1953, Moscow)
Russian-Soviet artist, co-founder and theorist of Constructivism. As fine artist Tatlin made a few paintings, but soon went over to three dimensional construction (contra-reliefs from 1913). On the architectural scene, he propagated an "Engineer's Art" which would combine constructive society-friendly functionality with revolutionary forms. This engineer's art culminated in the swivelling spiral tower "Monument of the third International" which was planned as a congress building (1919/20, never realised). In 1929/30 Tatlin started the construction of a flying bi-cycle. With his pioneering ideas Tatlin was way ahead of his time.

Teodoro, Franco, (born 1939, Turin)
See Gatti, Piero

Thonet GmbH
This cabinet maker (today Thonet Brothers GmbH) which was established in 1819 by Michael Thonet in Boppard is one of the most famous furniture makers in the world. Their fame was based on Michael Thonet's idea to manufacture furniture from bent wood into shapes which up to then had not been possible. A well-known example is the café chair (today model "No !4") of 1859, which acted as prototype for industrial furniture. In 1848 the firm moved to Vienna where they worked together with the secessionists such as Josef Hoffmann and Otto Wagner ("post office bank chair" 1904). Le Corbusier furnished the Paris art deco exhibition of 1925 with Thonet chairs; from 1928 Marcel Breuer's steel tube furniture "B35" was produced. In 1939 Thonet signed a contract with Ludwig Mies van der Rohe and obtained the licence for his free-swinging chair of 1932. In 1945 the firm resettled in Frankenberg/Eder, Hessen, and continued its co-operation with well-known artists such as Peter Maly and Norman Foster ("S900F",1999).

Tiffany, Louis Comfort (18.2.1848, New York–17.1.1933, New York)
American craftsman, trained as painter. Tiffany was the most important representative of American art nouveau. In 1879 he established the " Tiffany Glass and Decorating Company"; his table lamps, made according to a special process, iridescent "Favrille-Glass", were already treasures in Tiffany's life-time and receive the highest prices today. He also made jewellery, furniture, textiles and wallpaper. After the death of his father, Charles Louis (1812–1902) died, he took over the shop Tiffany & Co. in New York.

Velde, Henry Clemens van de (3.4.1863, Antwerp–27.10.1957, Zurich)

Belgian architect, artist and furniture designer. Van de Velde's influence on the German Jugendstil was enormous; not only has his characteristically curved architecture considerably affected the German Jugendstil, but equally so his domestic appliances, furniture and interiors, his typographical work and book decorations. In 1907 he was one of the cofounders of the German Worker's Union (1907). From 1906–1914 he led the newly established craftsman's school in Weimar which later became the Bauhaus (van de Velde recommended Walter Gropius as his successor).

Volkswagen

The car manufacturer, nowadays Volkswagen AG in Wolfsburg, was established in 1938 for the production of the "power-through-joy-car" which Ferdinand Porsche had developed from 1934. In the fifties this VW Beetle became a national symbol for the re-building of Germany and also for the mobility of a new middle class. The round form that Ferdinand Porsche developed was streamlined by the Porsche car body designer Erwin Komenda – the so-called tongue at the rear and front, rounded cross-beams and voluminous fenders which gave it its unmistakable shape and already in 1938 caused the New York Times to jokingly referred to it as a "beetle". A new edition of the "Beetle" design and myth is the "New Beetle" which has been produced by Volkswagen AG since 1994.

Wagenfeld, Wilhelm (15.4.1900, Bremen–28.5.1990, Stuttgart)

German industrial designer. Wagenfeld had given himself completely to designing and one of his first works already became famous, the "Table lamp" with milk glass dome and glass base, which the Bauhaus student Laszlo Moholy-Nagy designed. From 1926 Wagenfeld was assistant in the metal workshop at the Bauhaus, and in 1928 he took over as its leader. From 1930 he worked for himself but also taught at various higher institutions such as the College for Fine Arts in Berlin. In 1954 he opened his own workplace in Stuttgart (closed 1978). With his "Tea pot" of 1923 for Jenaer Glass and his glass "cube crockery" (1938, for the Vereinigte Lausitzer Glaswerke). Wagenfeld made design history with his salt and pepper pots "Max und Moritz" (1953, for WMF) and the portable radio "Combi" (for Braun, 1954) The name Wagenfeld stands for the idea of quality without compromise – functional, affordable and aesthetically pleasing, for all products of the industry.

Wagner, Otto (13.7.1841, Penzing–11.4.1918, Vienna)

Austrian architect, furniture designer and city planner. As developer of "Nutzstil" – architecture that is governed by construction and material – Wagner became the father of the Austrian Moderns; an entire generation of architects were taught by him, such as Josef Hoffmann, Adolf Loos and Joseph Maria Olbrich. His furniture designs came as a result of large building commissions like the Vienna Ring, the city train or the post office savings bank, for which he designed the famous "Postsparkassenstuhl" (1904, manufactured by Thonet).

Webb, Philip Speakman (12.1.1831, Oxford–17.4.1915, Worth/Sussex)

British architect, interior designer and craftsman. Webb was an important exponent of the style called "Vernacular Revival" (around 1860–1900) which enjoyed close relations with the Arts-and-Crafts movement. In 1859–1860 Webb built the "Red House" in Bexley Heath near London, a simple connected construction of red bricks with roof that extended down low, for William Morris. For Morris' firm Webb designed various interiors, furniture, textiles and glass windows.

Vienna Secession

In the era of Jugendstil, artists from many places joined forces to realise their special programmes and goals, such as the Munich Secession with Franz von Stuck (established in 1892) or the Berlin Secession which originated from the Group of Eleven which was founded in 1892 by Max Liebermann. The most important association was, however, the Vienna Secession with Gustav Klimt, Koloman Moser and Joseph Maria Olbrich who gave the Austrian variants the name "Secessionsstil". The Vienna work place (1903) which was established by Hoffmann and Moser with the aid of the banker Fritz Wärndorfer manufactured pieces of the highest artistic quality for all wakes of life in geometrical Secession style.

Wright, Frank Lloyd (8.6.1869, Richland Centre – 9.4.1959, Phoenix)

American architect. Wright's idea of the organic interaction of interior and nature had a lasting influence on the architecture of the 20th century. A good example is the villa "Falling Water House" in Bear Run (1927–1939) which has been erected directly over a waterfall. Wright's office and industrial buildings of stone, steel, reinforced concrete and glass are characterised by statics and the precise use of materials. One of his main works is the Guggenheim Museum in New York (1956–1959)

Zanotta

The furniture factory Zanotta was established in 1954 by Aurelio Zanotta. With the armchair minus frame "Throw Away", manufactured by Willie Landels, the firm changed over to the production of designer furniture and became one of the most important platforms for the Italian avant-garde design. Early successes were the inflatable chair "Blow" (by De Pas, D'Urbino. Lomazzi, 1968) and the bean bag "Sacco 9" (by Gatti, Paolini, Teodoro, 1968/69). An impressive row of well-known designers work for Zanotta. Beside those already mentioned Achille Castiglioni, Paolo Deganello, Enzo Mari, Alessandro Mendini and Ettore Sottsass design upholstered furniture, tables, chairs and household objects.

Zanuso, Marco (born 14.5.1916, Milan)

Italian architect, furniture and industrial designer. Zanuso is a wonderful example of that designer generation in Italy in the sixties, who was looking for solutions to combine art and technique, aesthetics and functionality in an optimal way. Zanosu, one of the founders of the Italian industrial design, invented some of the most wonderful solutions to shaping: initiated by the portable radio "TS 502", a tip-up cube with rounded corners which he made together with Richard Sapper in 1964, the televisions for the firm Brionvega (1964–1969, also with Richard Sapper) with their completely new design up to the table "Laveno" for Zanotta (1986). In later years Zanuso dedicated himself afresh to architecture.